AQA

GCSE (9–1)

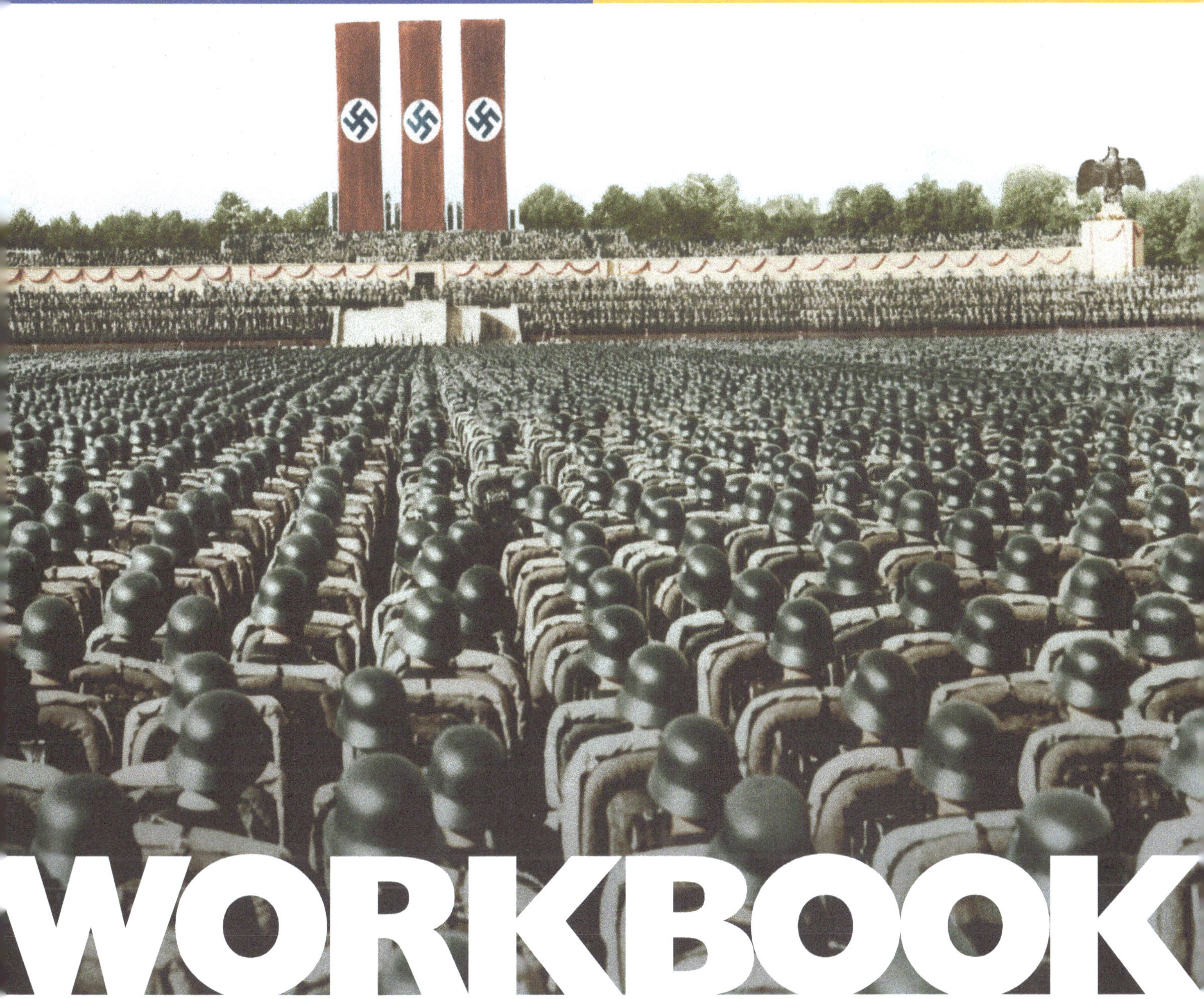

WORKBOOK

History

Germany 1890–1945: democracy and dictatorship

Adele Fletcher

Series editor: David Ferriby

Contents

Topic 1: Germany and the growth of democracy
- Kaiser Wilhelm and the difficulties of ruling Germany 3
- Impact of the First World War 7
- Weimar democracy: political change and unrest 13

Topic 2: Germany and the Depression
- The impact of the Depression 18
- The failure of Weimar democracy 23
- The establishment of Hitler's dictatorship 26

Topic 3: The experiences of Germans under the Nazis
- Economic changes 32
- Social policy and practice 38
- Control 43

---

1 This workbook will help you to prepare for the **AQA GCSE Germany, 1890–1945: democracy and dictatorship** Paper 1 exam.

2 Your **Paper 1 exam** is 1 hour and 45 minutes long. You will be assessed on your Period Study (GCSE Germany, 1890–1945: Democracy and dictatorship) and on your Wider World Depth Study. In total there are 84 marks available for this paper, which makes up 50% of your GCSE.

3 Section A, the Period Study, is divided into six compulsory questions, worth 40 marks in total. You are advised to spend 50 minutes on this section.

4 Questions 1–3 of Section A are **interpretation questions**. You will need to read the interpretations booklet very carefully and use the interpretations supported with contextual knowledge in your answers.

5 Questions 4–6 require you to use your **contextual knowledge** of the period. Read the dates given in the question carefully and ensure your answers are relevant.

6 This workbook will help you to become familiar with the knowledge required for this examination, as well as developing your understanding of how to answer the six different types of question.

7 For each topic there are:
- stimulus materials including key terms and concepts
- short-answer questions that build up to exam-style questions
- spaces provided for you to write or plan your answers

8 You still need to read your textbook and refer to your class notes, and possibly a revision guide.

9 **Timings** are given for the exam-style questions to make your practice as realistic as possible.

10 **Marks** available are indicated for all exam-style questions so that you can gauge the level of detail required in your answers.

11 Answers are available at: www.hoddereducation.co.uk/workbookanswers

Germany and the growth of democracy

Kaiser Wilhelm and the difficulties of ruling Germany

1. Complete the table below to show at least two problems and/or limitations for each of those who had political power in Germany between 1890 and 1914. One example has been included to help you get started.

Ruling power	Problems/limitations
Kaiser, Wilhelm II	Left-wing political parties were slowly gaining more support. They championed the rights of workers and wanted a reduction in the Kaiser's power.
Chancellor	
Reichstag	

2. Circle accurate statements about Prussia in the 1890s.

Prussia was the most important state within Germany.	Prussia wanted to join with Germany's closest countries, including France.	Prussia had two-thirds of the population and over half of Germany's territory.
Prussia appointed the Reichstag.	Prussian military leaders often determined German foreign policy.	Prussian leaders wanted a strong air force.

3. In three words summarise who held power in Germany in 1890.

4. Read the following statements about political parties. Identify points relating to right-wing political parties with an R, and points defining left-wing political parties with an L.
   - Support traditional values
   - Nationalistic
   - Support the rights of the worker
   - Demand social reforms such as old age pensions
   - Promote the rights of the landowners
   - Mainly supported by industrial workers

5. a Which party did the growing number of industrial workers mostly support in Germany in the late 1800s and early 1900s?

   ....

   b State three reasons why industrial workers supported the party.

   ....
   ....
   ....

6. State three reasons why Kaiser Wilhelm II wanted a strong German navy.

   ....
   ....
   ....
   ....

7. Complete the table to give an overview of the first two German naval laws.

Naval law	Year passed	Details
First Naval Law		
Second Naval Law		

8 Write a description of the impact of industrialisation on Germany between 1890 and 1914. It should be approximately one paragraph long. You must include the following words:

| rapid | steel | Britain |
| industry | export | growth of cities |

Exam-style questions

9 Describe two problems facing the growth of parliamentary government before 1914.

5 | 4 marks

10 In what ways did Kaiser Wilhelm II affect domestic policy in the years before the First World War broke out? Ensure you cover at least two consequences and support them with specific factual knowledge.

10 **8 marks**

....

11 Which of the following was the more important reason why domestic naval laws were passed in Germany from 1898? Explain your answer with reference to both reasons, with supporting factual information and a clear conclusion.
- Kaiser Wilhelm II's desire to build an empire
- to rival the British navy

15 **12 marks**

....

Impact of the First World War

12 The following key words relate to the First World War. Match them to the correct explanation.

Key word	Explanation
Abdication	Getting rid of military weapons and forces
War guilt	Term used in Germany to describe the Treaty of Versailles
Kaiser	Giving up the throne
Hyperinflation	Payment of money for the cost of the First World War
Diktat	The population votes for its government in regular elections
Disarmament	Clause 231 of the Treaty of Versailles which blamed Germany and her allies for the First World War
Reparation	Prices of goods increase rapidly as inflation accelerates and goes out of control
Republic	End of fighting in a war to allow peace talks to start
Armistice	Problems in the economy that lead to lower living standards
Democracy	Emperor of Germany
Economic depression	Country with no hereditary leader. The people and elected representatives hold power

13 Using the following words, write a paragraph about the impact of defeat in the First World War on Germany in 1918.

| economic | society | political | problems | divisions |

| war weariness | gap | anger | abdication |

....
....
....
....
....
....
....

14 Tick the statements below to identify if they are true or false about the abdication of the Kaiser in November 1918.

Statement	True	False
The Kaiser was unwilling to abdicate. He was forced to leave.		
The Kaiser was on the battlefield in France leading his soldiers when he abdicated.		
German sailors, soldiers and workers' councils had full faith in the Kaiser and were willing to support and protect him when he abdicated.		
Politicians and military leaders encouraged the Kaiser to abdicate.		
The Kaiser abdicated on 9 November 1918.		

15 Give two examples of the impact of the Treaty of Versailles on the following sectors in Germany. The first has been completed for you.

Sector	Impact of the Treaty of Versailles
Military	Army was limited to 100,000 men Conscription banned
Land	
Population	
Industry	
Alliances	

16 a Complete the diagram to show the structure of the Weimar constitution. You need to insert the following terms: president, German people, chancellor, armed forces, Reichstag, courts.

```
                         ┌──────────────────┐
                         │                  │
          Appointed      │    Appointed     │      Controlled
          judges         ▼                  ▼
      ┌──────────┐     ┌──────────┐      ┌──────────┐
      │          │     │          │      │          │
      └──────────┘     └──────────┘      └──────────┘
                            │
                            │ Appointed
                            ▼
                     ┌──────────────┐
                     │ Government    │
                     │ ministers     │
                     └──────────────┘

                                              ┌──────────────────────────────┐
                                              │ 17 local governments.        │
                                              │ The constitution limited     │
                      ┌──────────────┐        │ their authority.             │
                      │              │        └──────────────────────────────┘
   Elected            └──────────────┘
                         ▲ Elected                   ▲ Elected
      ┌─────────────────────────────────────────────────────┐
      │                                                     │
      └─────────────────────────────────────────────────────┘
```

b Using the terms you have added to the diagram as a starting point, make some notes on the strengths and weaknesses of the constitution.

....
....
....
....
....
....
....
....
....
....

17 Put the following events relating to the invasion of the Ruhr in chronological order. The first event has been done for you.

Events	Chronological order
Germany paid the first reparation instalment in 1921.	1
French and Belgian troops entered the Ruhr.	
The Germans told the French government they were unable to meet reparation repayments. The French did not believe them.	
The French took raw materials and goods as a substitute for the failed reparation repayment.	
The German currency collapsed.	
The French government sent in its own workers to the Ruhr.	
Germany failed to pay the second reparation repayment in 1922.	
Violence broke out. German police officers and workers were arrested.	
The German government ordered workers in the Ruhr to offer passive resistance.	

18 Complete the table to show the impact of hyperinflation on different sectors of society. The first row has been completed for you as an example.

Sectors of society	Impact: good/bad	Explanation
Very wealthy landowners	good	They were protected as land was a possession. Also, they often held money in foreign currencies and had other possessions.
Middle class with savings		
Farmers		
Pensioners		
Poor with debts		

19 Complete the spider diagram to summarise the situation in Weimar Germany in 1923. Include at least two more specific examples for domestic politics and foreign relations.

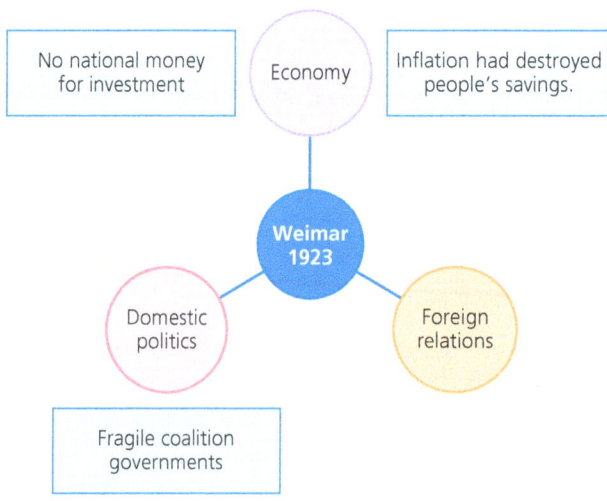

20 a Complete the diamond nine to show the extent to which different factors weakened the Weimar Republic up to 1923. Place the factor that you believed weakened it the most at the top.

Factors
- i Distrust of politicians
- ii Invasion of the Ruhr
- iii Armistice
- iv Public opinion of Friedrich Ebert
- v Military restrictions imposed by the Treaty of Versailles
- vi Reparation repayments not paid, 1922
- vii Reparation repayments imposed by the Treaty of Versailles
- viii Territorial losses from the Treaty of Versailles
- ix Extremist parties leading rebellions

b Explain your top and bottom decisions using relevant information you have learned.

Exam-style questions

Interpretation A

The impact of hyperinflation within Germany was uneven. Some profited from it. Adroit speculators like the tycoon Hugo Stinnes made fortunes, and industrialists and landowners who owed money were able to pay off their debts in devalued currency. Others were able to escape the worst — those, for example, whose wealth took the form of property or those with goods or skills which could be readily bartered.

Alan White, *The Weimar Republic* (1997)

Interpretation B

We were out playing football and one of my friends said: 'I'm going to the shop to buy a couple of bread rolls.'...he had a 500,000 mark note... But he only came back with one, because a roll now cost 400,000 marks.

The memories of Karl Nagerl, who was a schoolboy in 1923

21 How does Interpretation B differ from Interpretation A about the impact of hyperinflation on the people of Germany in 1923? Explain your answer based on what it says in Interpretations A and B.

[4 marks]

22 Why might the authors of Interpretations A and B have different interpretations of the impact of hyperinflation on the people of Germany in 1923? Explain your answer using the two interpretations and your contextual knowledge.

[4 marks]

23 Which interpretation gives the more convincing opinion about the impact of hyperinflation on the people of Germany in 1923? Explain your answer based on your contextual knowledge and what it says in Interpretations A and B. **10 8 marks**

Plan your answer below. You can write your answer on a separate piece of paper.

....
....
....
....
....
....
....
....

Weimar democracy: political change and unrest

24 a Complete the table on manifestations of political unrest up to 1923.

Unrest	Date	Details	Outcome
Spartacists			
Kapp Putsch			
Munich Putsch			

Germany and the growth of democracy

13

b For each uprising, write a sentence or two explaining how significant a threat it posed to the Weimar government.

....
....
....
....
....
....
....
....

25 Complete the table to provide examples of Weimar's recovery 1924–29. One row has been completed for you.

Aspect of recovery	Details	How it helped Weimar to recover	Chronological order
Entry to the League of Nations			
Dawes Plan	1924: USA loaned Weimar 800 million marks. Agreed that reparation repayments could be spread over a longer period.	Weimar government had money to invest in industry and in turn create jobs.	2
Introduction of the Rentenmark			
Young Plan			
Locarno Treaty			

26 a Read the following statements and identify whether they are examples of financial improvement or decline.

Sector	Financial situation 1924–early 1929	Improvement or decline?
Steel industry	Germany's industrial production increased. The steel industry, along with the chemical industry, made up nearly half of all industrial output. By 1928 levels of production had returned to pre-war levels.	
Large landowners	Value of land rose. For example, land values in Berlin rose over 700%.	
Industrial workers	Unions were allowed under Weimar governments. Increasing production led to increased pay.	
Farmers	Farmers had greatly benefited during the First World War as imports had reduced. However, after the war farmers were overproducing.	
Small business owners	The opening of large department stores threatened many small businesses.	

b Plot changes in the financial position of these sectors above on the continuum line below and justify your judgement. An example has been completed for you.

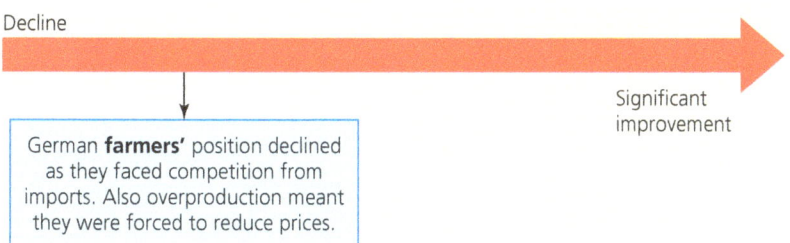

Decline → Significant improvement

German **farmers'** position declined as they faced competition from imports. Also overproduction meant they were forced to reduce prices.

27 Add two specific points for each heading on the spider diagram to show the cultural revival of Weimar during the 1920s.

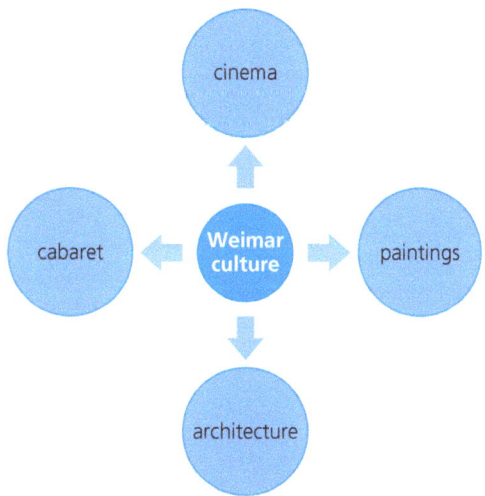

28 a How stable was the Weimar Republic in 1929? Highlight statements which suggest the Weimar Republic had been recovering by 1929 in green. Highlight statements which suggest the Weimar Republic was doomed by 1929 in pink.

- There were no attempted political coups from 1925.
- Weimar's economic recovery was based on loans from America that could be recalled at any time.
- In 1928 moderate parties had 136 more seats in the Reichstag than radical parties.
- By 1928 Germany's level of production was the same as in 1913, before the start of the First World War.
- Unemployment was rising in 1928. It was 6% in 1928.

b In the table below, add two further examples for each side of the debate using your own knowledge.

Weimar Republic recovering by 1929	Weimar Republic was doomed by 1929

Exam-style questions

29 Describe two problems that the Weimar government faced between 1919 and 1923. **5** **4 marks**

30 In what ways did the lives of people in Germany change during Weimar's 'golden years', from 1924 to 1929? Explain your answer. (10) **8 marks**

31 Which of the following was the more important reason why Weimar started to recover in the years from 1924 to early 1929? Explain your answer, referring to both reasons and using specific factual knowledge. Make sure you reach a clear judgement.

- Loans from America: the Dawes and Young Plans
- International treaties including the Locarno Treaty

(10) **12 marks**

Plan your answer below. You can write your answer on a separate piece of paper.

Germany and the Depression

The impact of the Depression

1 a Tick the statements below to identify if they are true or false about the impact of the Depression on Germany between 1929 and 1932.

Impact of the Depression on Germany	True	False
Unemployment rose to 13 million.		
Germany experienced hyperinflation in the year 1931.		
All sectors of German society were affected by the Depression.		
Reparation repayments were still demanded by Allies, putting Germany under more economic pressure.		
The German chancellor increased taxes, cut wages and reduced unemployment benefit.		
The USA continued to loan Germany money during the Depression.		

b Change the false statements to make them true about the situation in Germany during the Depression.

....

....

....

....

2 Give one example of the impact of the Depression on each sector of German society. The first has been completed for you.

Sector of society	Impact of the Depression
Business owners	Many businesses closed as people could not afford to buy their products. Those that did not close experienced a fall in profit.
Young people	
Farmers	
Industrial workers	

3 a For each factor below, briefly explain how it led to an increase in support for the Nazi Party in the years 1929–32.

Factor	How it helped attract more support for the Nazi Party
i Distrust of Weimar politicians and Heinrich Brüning's economic policy	
ii Wall Street Crash	
iii Communist threat	
iv The appeal of Adolf Hitler	
v Restrictions imposed by the Treaty of Versailles	
vi The SA	
vii Nazi propaganda	
viii Unemployment	
ix Nazi 25-point programme	

b   Complete the diamond nine to show the extent to which different factors increased support for the Nazi Party between 1929 and 1932. Place the factor that you believe attracted most support at the top.

c   Explain your top and bottom decisions using specific examples.

....
....
....
....

4   Using the graph on the right, answer the following questions.

a   What happened to Communist support between 1928 and November 1932?

....
....

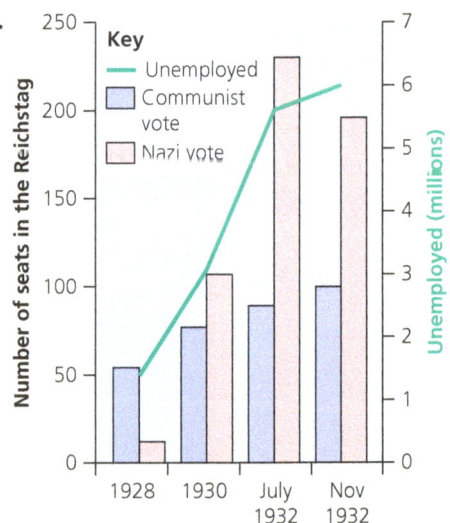

b   Describe Nazi Party success in Reichstag elections from 1928 to July 1932.

....
....
....

c   What happened to Nazi Party seats between July 1932 and the November 1932 election?

....
....

d   Why did increasing numbers of Germans vote for extreme political parties between 1928 and 1932?

....
....

5 For each of the statements below, mark with either SA or SS depending on whether they describe:

SA: the stormtroopers of the Nazi Party, or

SS: the protection squad of the Nazi Party

- Protected Nazi rallies and disrupted opponents' political meetings
- Members known as the Brownshirts
- Led by Heinrich Himmler
- Swore total loyalty to Hitler
- Led by Ernst Röhm
- After 1934 were the main instrument of terror in Nazi Germany
- Lacked discipline
- Members known as the Blackshirts

Exam-style questions

Interpretation A

Hitler's success was undoubtedly due to the Great Depression. Yet the Nazi Party made the most of the situation and appealed to the German people on two levels.

1. Its appeal to the whole nation, on issues that concerned everyone.

2. It also appealed to sectors of the population, on issues that affected them separately.

S. J. Lee, *Weimar and Nazi Germany*, 1996.

Interpretation B

It seemed as if he [Hitler] was candidly presenting his anxieties about the future. His irony was softened by a somewhat self-conscious humour; his south German charm reminded me agreeably of my native region...He spoke urgently and with hypnotic persuasiveness. The mood he cast was much deeper than the speech itself. Moreover, I was carried on the wave of enthusiasm which bore the speaker along from sentence to sentence.

Albert Speer, *Inside the Third Reich*, first published in 1969.

(*Inside the Third Reich* is a memoir written by Albert Speer, who was Nazi minister of armaments from 1942 to 1945 and who served Hitler throughout his time in power. Speer was sentenced to 20 years in prison after his 1945 trial.

6 How does Interpretation B differ from Interpretation A about the appeal of Hitler in Germany? Explain your answer based on what it says in Interpretations A and B.

(5) **4 marks**

7 Why might the authors of Interpretations A and B have different interpretations of the appeal of Hitler? Explain your answer using Interpretations A and B and your contextual knowledge.

(5 minutes, 4 marks)

8 Which interpretation gives the more convincing opinion about the appeal of Hitler in Germany? Explain your answer based on your contextual knowledge and what it says in Interpretations A and B.

(10 minutes, 8 marks)

The failure of Weimar democracy

9 Match the description of Nazi Party experiences in Reichstag elections to the correct election date.

Description	Election date
The Nazis continued to be the largest party. Nevertheless, it was a bad election for them, as they lost 34 seats.	July 1932
Hitler gained the most votes in the Reichstag and therefore the largest number of seats, 288. This was not enough for a majority and he had to join with the smaller Nationalist Party, which had 52 seats.	November 1932
The Nazi Party won 230 seats. Hitler demanded to be appointed chancellor.	March 1933

10 Add one further fact for each of the key individuals involved in German politics between 1932 and 1933.

a **President Hindenburg**
His main advisers were rich conservative industrialists
....

b **Heinrich Brüning**
Unpopular chancellor
....

c **General von Schleicher**
Distrusted Hitler
....

d **Franz von Papen**
Rich Catholic
....

11 Number the events leading to Hitler becoming chancellor in chronological order.

November 1932:
- Nazis are the largest single party but their share of the vote has fallen.
- Hindenburg refuses to appoint Hitler as chancellor.

Hitler is appointed chancellor on 30 January 1933.

Reichstag election, July 1932:
- Nazi Party voted the largest single party but failed to secure a majority.
- Hitler demands to be chancellor. President Hindenburg refuses and von Papen remains chancellor.

Kurt von Schleicher is appointed chancellor.

Von Papen has little support in the Reichstag and calls an election.

Hindenburg and von Papen meet in secret with industrialists, army leaders and politicians.

Von Schleicher is forced to resign as chancellor.

12 Explain how Hitler and the Nazi Party appealed to each section of the population to try to gain their votes in Reichstag elections.

Sector of society	How Hitler and the Nazi Party appealed to them
Rich large business owners	Promised to remove trade unions and to invest in the German economy, creating more business.
Middle class	
Working class	

13 a Create a list of 10 reasons why Hitler became chancellor in January 1933.

....

....

....

....

....

....

....

....

....

....

b Colour code your reasons:
- Yellow: Nazi strengths/tactics
- Blue: weaknesses of the Weimar Republic and politicians
- Pink: Wall Street Crash and its impact

c Rank the reasons in what you think is the order of importance.

d Justify the reason you placed at the top using specific evidence.

....

....

....

....

....

....

....

Exam-style questions

14 Describe two economic problems faced by the Weimar Republic between 1930 and 1932.

(5) 4 marks

15 In what ways did the lives of people in Germany change as a consequence of the Great Depression? Explain your answer.

(10) 8 marks

16 Which of the following was the more important reason why Hitler was appointed chancellor of Germany in 1933? Explain your answer with reference to both factors.

- Nazi strengths
- the political weakness of the Weimar Republic

(15) 12 marks

Answer on a separate piece of paper. Use the space below to plan your answer.

The establishment of Hitler's dictatorship

17 Complete the following quick-fire questions on the Reichstag fire.

a   What was the date of the Reichstag fire?

b   Which political party did Hitler blame for starting the fire?

c   Who was arrested at the scene of the fire?

d   Who gave Hitler emergency powers following the fire?

e   Which political party did Hitler target with the emergency powers?

18 The following statements are all about the events following the Reichstag fire. However, each one contains a mistake.

a   Underline the mistake.
b   Correct the mistake on the line below the statement.

- The night after the fire, Göring's police arrested and imprisoned 4,000 Communist leaders.

- Hitler declared that members of the German National People's Party posed a danger to Germany.

- On 25 March Hitler persuaded President Hindenburg to pass an emergency decree.

- Hindenburg used Article 46 to pass the emergency decree.

- The emergency decree guaranteed all personal liberties and freedoms of press, assembly and speech.

- Himmler's police used the decree to ban meetings, close newspapers and remove the opposition.

- Göring's police seized all state newspapers.

- The emergency decree lasted 12 months, until Hitler became Führer.

19 Within six months of becoming chancellor, Adolf Hitler had eliminated political opposition.

a   Complete the timeline by inserting details of Hitler's actions in the first half of 1933.
b   For each action, briefly explain how it helped the Nazis create a dictatorship.
c   Highlight actions to show whether they involved:
- use of force (highlight in yellow)
- use of the law against opponents (highlight in blue)
- making deals with opponents or potential opponents (highlight in green)

Date	Action	How this helped the Nazi Party gain control
30 January	Hitler appointed chancellor	Lead position in the Reichstag, able to appoint Nazis into the cabinet.
27 February	Reichstag fire	
28 February		
5 March		
13 March	Goebbels took control of German media	
24 March		
April	Civil service, law courts and education purged of Nazi opposition	
2 May		
14 July		
20 July	Concordat with the Catholic Church	

20 a Read the statements below about the Night of the Long Knives. Using different colours, highlight the statements according to which heading you would group them under.

　　i　Reasons for the purge

　　ii　Events of the Night of the Long Knives, 29–30 June 1934

　　iii　Impact of the Night of the Long Knives

- Hitler removed potential opponents.
- During the weekend of 29–30 June 1934, leaders of the SS arrested leaders of the SA and other possible opponents of Hitler. This included von Schleicher.
- The SA was increasingly out of control at a time when Hitler was trying to establish a dictatorship through legal methods.
- The SA's numbers and influence were heavily reduced.
- After Hindenburg died in August 1934, the army leaders swore an oath of allegiance to Hitler, giving him their unconditional obedience.
- Leading Nazis were concerned about Röhm's growing influence and power within the Nazi Party.
- The official number killed during the purge is 76, but historians estimate it to be much higher.
- In the summer of 1934, the number of men in the SA had reached nearly 2 million. They were under the leadership of Röhm.
- Himmler wanted to replace the SA with his own SS.
- The regular army was worried Röhm would take it over and merge it with the SA. Röhm had stated that this was his intention.
- Hitler believed Röhm was a threat.

b Write a chronological account of the Night of the Long Knives using your highlighted statements.

21 Quick-fire questions:

a The date Hindenburg died.

b What position did Hitler award himself within hours of Hindenburg's death?

c Which of the two actions below did Hitler immediately take?
- required the whole army to swear an oath of loyalty to him
- invaded France
- took the title of Führer, supreme leader
- ordered Kristallnacht

22 Match key words to correct definitions.

Key word	Definition
Article 48	a German word meaning leader
Chancellor	protection squad of the Nazi Party, also known as the Blackshirts
Concordat	an agreement or treaty between the Pope and a government, relating to matters of mutual interest
Depression	a government where one person or a small number of people make all the decisions
Dictatorship	head of state
Führer	an article of the constitution of the Weimar Republic of Germany which allowed the president, under certain circumstances, to take emergency measures without the prior consent of the Reichstag
Oath	a binding promise or appeal to a god or to some revered person or thing
Opponents	head of government
President	a person or group who disagrees with or resists a proposal or practice
Reichstag	period of financial problems that affects living standards
SA	Stormtroopers, also known as the Brownshirts
SS	parliament

23 a Complete the diamond nine to show how different factors led to Hitler becoming dictator. Place the factor that you think was most important at the top.

i appointed chancellor
ii Reichstag fire
iii March 1933 Reichstag election
iv Enabling Act
v trade unions banned
vi Law Against the Formation of New Parties
vii concordat
viii Night of the Long Knives
ix death of Hindenburg

b Explain your top and bottom decisions using specific examples.

....
....
....
....
....

Exam-style questions

Interpretation A

On the afternoon of 28 June, I asked SA Commander Heines to come and see me; I told him to his face that I knew of his preparations and I gave him a warning. He replied that he knew all about my measures and had thought that they were preparations for an attack on the SA. He had only put the SA on alert in order to resist an attack. He gave his word as an officer and SA leader that he had not planned or prepared any surprise attack upon the Army.

During the night of 28–29 June, Heines rang me up again. He had just learned that the Army throughout the Reich was on the alert for an SA putsch. I said to him that 'I have the impression that we — Army and SA — are being egged on against each other by a third party.' By that I mean Himmler.

After the war, Edward von Kleist of the German army recalled the events of June, 1934. From James Pool, *Who Financed Hitler: The Secret Funding of Hitler's Rise to Power* (1979), pp. 426–27. Reprinted with permission of Pocket Books, Simon & Schuster

Interpretation B

Hitler entered Röhm's bedroom alone with a whip in his hand. Behind him were two detectives with pistols at the ready. He spat out the words: 'Röhm, you are under arrest.'

Now the bus arrives. Quickly, the SA leaders are collected from the laundry room and walk past Röhm under police guard. Röhm looks up from his coffee sadly and waves to them in a melancholy way. At last Röhm too is led from the hotel. He walks past Hitler with his head bowed, completely apathetic.

Erich Kempka was Hitler's chauffeur on 29 June 1934. In 1946 he gave an interview in which he described what happened when Hitler arrived at the Hotel Hanselmayer that night. Taken from Arthur Schweitzer, *Big Business in the Third Reich* (1964), p. 37

24 How does Interpretation B differ from Interpretation A about the events of the Night of the Long Knives? Explain your answer based on what it says in Interpretations A and B.

5 **4 marks**

....
....
....
....
....
....

25 Why might the authors of Interpretations A and B have different interpretations of the events of the Night of the Long Knives? Explain your answer using Interpretations A and B and your contextual knowledge.

⏱ 10   **4 marks**

26 Which interpretation gives the more convincing opinion about the about the events of the Night of the Long Knives? Explain your answer based on your contextual knowledge and what it says in Interpretations A and B.

⏱ 10   **8 marks**

The experiences of Germans under the Nazis

Economic changes

1 List three economic problems that Germany faced in 1933.

....

....

....

2 The following key words relate to the experiences of Germans under the Nazis. Match them to the correct explanation.

Key word / individual	Explanation
Public works projects	headed the German Labour Front
Autobahn	needing no outside help to meet the needs of the people, especially with regard to the production of food; also known as autarky
Dr Hjalmar Schacht	infrastructure projects, such as the building of schools, organised and financed by the government to create employment
Government finance	minister of the economy
Dr Robert Ley	money provided by the government to fund something
German Labour Front	KdF: provide workers with leisure opportunities
Rearmament	building new stocks of weapons
Volkswagen	DAF: managed discipline, wages and working hours
Strength through joy	people's car
Hermann Göring	senior politician in the Nazi Party, later led the Luftwaffe
Self-sufficiency	motorway

3 List three examples of public works programmes established by the Nazi Party.

....

....

....

4 a Read the paragraph below and highlight all the correct information about Hitler's rearmament programme.

In 1935 conscription was reintroduced in Germany. It was to allow the Nazi Party to rebuild the army and Germany's military strength. It had been banned by Kaiser Wilhelm II in 1914. In 1938 the Four-Year Plan was launched. Led by Göring, it was to get Germany ready for war. It was designed to make sure Germany had good international relations. Hitler also wanted to create an excellent German air force, to be known as the RAF. Rearmament led to increased trade and business, as weapons and equipment for fighting were needed. This helped create more jobs and reduced unemployment. Although this was not a target of the Nazi Party, it pleased them. Jobs were created in department stores, butchers and coal mines. A key aim was to make Germany self-sufficient and war ready.

b Rewrite inaccurate sentences to make them correct.

....

....

....

....

5 Read the following statements about the Reich Labour Service (RAD). Tick to show if they are true or false.

Reich Labour Service (RAD)	True	False
Reich Labour Service Act passed July 1935		
Everybody aged 16–40 forced to join		
Complete six months' training		
Wear military uniform		
No wages		
Live in own home		
Perform physical exercise every day		

6 Write one paragraph about the reason for the establishment of the German Labour Front (DAF) and its impact on working conditions, using the following words.

| trade unions | DAF | banned | discipline |

| wages | control | working hours |

....

....

....

....

....

....

7 The following statements are all about Strength through Joy (KdF). Highlight in two different colours statements that relate to: i) its purpose; ii) activities it established or made cheaply and widely available.

- keep workers happy
- provide leisure activities
- cheap cruise holidays
- remove social barriers
- control workers
- sports activities
- trips to the cinema
- encourage people to support the Führer

8 a Complete the table to show the benefits and drawbacks of Nazi economic policies for specific groups in society. Include at least one benefit and drawback for each sector.

Sector	Benefits	Drawback
Big business	Rearmament led to increased trade and profits Removal of trade unions German industry grew in size and profitability	Government took control of wages and profits Government decided which businesses would have access to valuable resources
Middle class		
Farmers		
Industrial workers		

b Number the sectors in order of who you think benefited most from Nazi policies.

c Explain your decision about who benefited the most.

....
....
....
....
....

9 Which statement most accurately describes the German population's reaction to the outbreak of the Second World War in September 1939?

- The announcement of war was greeted by cheering crowds, similarly to the First World War. Hitler had prepared Germany, and the German people supported him in his policy of destroying the Allies.
- The German population was very happy at the outbreak of the Second World War. They wanted to defeat Britain and its allies. They fully supported the decision to invade Poland.
- The German people were not enthusiastic for war. They still had memories of defeat and hardship following Germany's defeat in the First World War. The population accepted it and were encouraged to support it through Nazi propaganda.
- The German people were angry at the outbreak of the Second World War. They did not support the decision and openly opposed Hitler's attack on Poland.

10 Match items rationed in Germany during the Second World War to the correct statement.

Item rationed	Statement
Food	Introduced in November 1939
Clothes	Not available
Hot water	Introduced in August 1939. Seven colour-coded ration cards were issued. Rationing made diets repetitive. Nevertheless, two out of five Germans ate better because of it
Toilet paper	Only children were entitled to it
Milk	Only permitted two days a week

11 Identify two groups in society that were entitled to extra rations, and explain briefly why each group had this entitlement.

....

....

....

....

....

....

12 The following statements are all about air raids on Germany. However, they all contain a mistake.

a Underline the mistake.
b Correct the mistake on the line below the statement.

- The first air raids on Berlin started in 1939.

  ....

- As air raids increased, Germans moved or were evacuated to urban areas.

  ....

- Before 1942 the British mainly targeted residential areas.

  ....

- Area bombing began in 1942 and targeted small cities.

  ....

- An estimated 5,000 people were killed by bombing raids.

  ....

- In late 1940 extreme air raids took place in Dresden. Nearly 70% of the city was destroyed.

  ....

- Around 2 million Germans were made homeless.

  ....

13 Read the following statements about the impact of the Second World War on employment in Germany. Tick to show if they are true or false.

Statement	True	False
Most German men were in the army, creating a labour shortage on the home front.		
Concentration camp prisoners were forced to work for the German war effort.		
Women were banned from entering the workforce.		
Prisoners of war were treated well to make sure they produced the best quality goods for the German war effort.		
Women worked in ammunition factories.		

14 Write one paragraph about the impact of war on Germany in terms of creating refugees. Include the following words in your answer.

air raids　　east　　west　　Russia armies

food shortages　　walk　　fled

Exam-style questions

15 Describe two problems faced by working-class Germans between 1933 and 1939. (5) **4 marks**

16 In what ways did the lives of people in Germany change as a consequence of the Second World War? Explain your answer. (10) **8 marks**

17 Which of the following benefited more from Nazi economic policies between 1933 and 1945? Explain your answer, referring to both categories and using specific factual knowledge. Make sure you reach a clear judgement.

- Farmers
- Big business

⏱ 15   **12 marks**

Plan your answer below and write it on a separate piece of paper.

....
....
....
....
....

Social policy and practice

18 For each school curriculum subject listed, briefly explain how it was taught to support Nazi Party policies and ideals.

- History

....
....
....

- Biology

....
....
....

- Maths

....
....
....

19 Complete the table to detail Nazi Party policies towards young people.

Group	Aims	Members	Activities
Hitler Youth			
League of German Maidens			

20. **Plot these Nazi policies towards the church on the timeline.**
    - Nazi campaign to discourage children from attending church schools and church youth groups.
    - Creation of the Reich Church, to unify all Protestant churches in one official Reich Church.
    - All religion in schools banned.
    - Concordat between the Nazi Party and Catholic church.
    - Christmas carols and plays banned from schools.

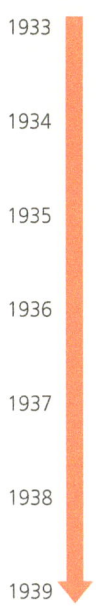

1933

1934

1935

1936

1937

1938

1939

21. **Circle the accurate statements representing Nazi attitudes towards women.**

| should have a family, the more children the better | should run their own businesses | should have a traditional role |
| should become leaders in the Nazi Party | should support their husbands | should hold high-ranking roles in the military |

22. **Translate the statement 'Kinder, Küche, Kirche'.**

....

....

23. **State two ways in which the Nazi Party encouraged their policy of 'Kinder, Küche, Kirche'.**

....

....

....

....

24. **Match the different social groups to the persecution they faced.**

Social group	Persecution
Sinti and Roma people	For individuals with a hereditary illness, sterilisation was enforced. In 1939 a programme of euthanasia started. At least 5,000 children were killed between 1939 and 1945, and 72,000 people with mental illnesses were gassed between 1939 and 1941.
Gay people	Five out of every six were killed with no public outcry. They were believed to be inferior people.
Disabled people	They were sent to concentration camps with no public outcry. They were seen as a threat to traditional family life.

The experiences of Germans under the Nazis

39

25 The following events arising from Nazi Party policies towards Jews are shown in the correct chronological order.
- Boycott of Jewish shops
- Nuremberg Laws
- Lull in anti-Semitic policy due to the Olympics
- Aryanisation of Jewish businesses increased
- Red 'J' stamped in all Jews' passports
- Kristallnacht
- Wannsee Conference

a Plot them in the correct year on the timeline below.

1933
1934
1935
1936
1937
1938
1939
1940
1941
1942
1943
1944
1945

b Briefly describe each event and its impact on Jews inside Nazi Germany.

....
....
....
....
....
....
....
....
....
....
....
....
....

26 Write one paragraph, using all the words below, to explain why the Nazi Party was able to increase its persecution of Jews and start the Final Solution.

| Second World War | Final Solution | invasion of Russia | Einsatzgruppen |

| ghettos | Poland | concentration and death camps |

Exam-style questions

Interpretation A

Until Kristallnacht, many Germans believed Hitler was not engaged in mass murder. [The treatment of the Jews] seemed to be a minor form of harassment of a disliked minority.

Alfons Heck, member of the Hitler Youth in 1938, interviewed for a television programme in 1989.

Interpretation B

The Gestapo in Cologne was exceptionally weak. The calm, elderly officers let things come to them and did not undertake any of their own initiatives...The Nuremberg Laws were well known at that time to all judges and attorneys. Today they are thought of as criminal. The Jews were placed outside of the German community because of the laws. This was indeed wrong, as I now know, but at the time it was the law of the land.

Dr Emanuel Schäfer on Tuesday 6 July 1954, the first day of his trial before a Cologne jury court for assisting in the deportation of the Cologne Jews to the death factories in the east in 1941 and 1942. He was a former leader of the Cologne Gestapo.

27 How does Interpretation B differ from Interpretation A about the treatment of Jews between 1933 and 1939? Explain your answer based on what it says in Interpretations A and B.

5 **4 marks**

28 Why might the authors of Interpretations A and B have different interpretations of the treatment of Jews between 1933 and 1939? Explain your answer using Interpretations A and B and your contextual knowledge. **(5) 4 marks**

29 Which interpretation gives the more convincing opinion about the treatment of Jews between 1933 and 1939? Explain your answer based on your contextual knowledge and what it says in Interpretations A and B. **(10) 8 marks**

Control

30 Read the following statements and tick to show if they are describing Joseph Goebbels or Heinrich Himmler.

Statement	Goebbels	Himmler
Head of Nazi propaganda		
Appointed minister for public enlightenment in 1933		
Became head of SS in 1929		
Role included eliminating opposition to the Nazi Party		
Used media to promote Nazi policies		
Carried out racial policies		

31 a Copy the spider diagram below onto a larger piece of paper (A4 is fine). Add two specific details to each of the different propaganda methods Goebbels used to increase Nazi control.

b For each method of propaganda add a strength and a limitation.

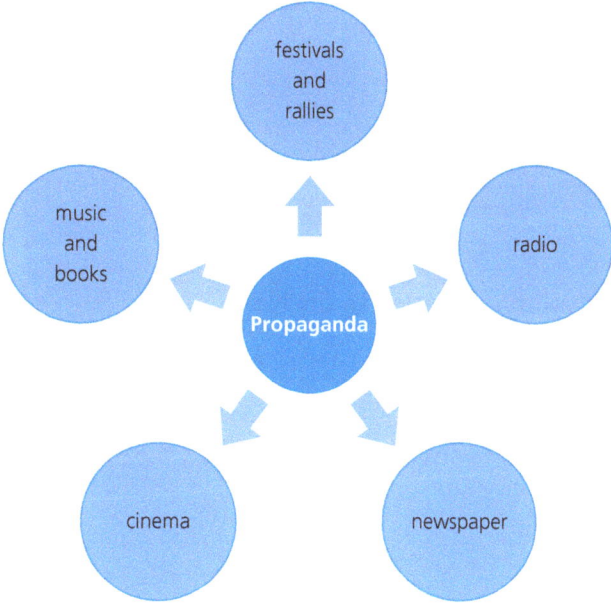

32 Read the following statements about the SS. Tick to show if they are true or false.

Statement	True	False
SS stands for Schutzstaffel: 'protection squad'.		
All members were Aryans — tall, blond, blue-eyed men.		
SS consisted of one unit with no subdivisions.		
Its main task was terror and intimidation.		
Following the outbreak of the Second World War the importance of the SS declined.		
The SS was a minor section of the Nazi Party.		

33 Complete the table to show how the Nazi Party controlled the German population.

Method of control	Purpose	Activities	How it helped secure Hitler's position
Gestapo	State secret police, designed to eliminate opposition.	Tapped telephones, spied on civilians, had a network of informers. Arrested people suspected of acting against the Nazi Party	Spread fear among the general population. Reduced open opposition to Hitler and the Nazis
Concentration camps			
Informers			
Police and courts			

34 a Complete the table on youth opposition to the Nazis.

Youth opposition group	Members	Anti-Nazi Party actions	Nazi Party reaction
Swing Youth			
Edelweiss Pirates			
White Rose Group			

b Number the youth opposition groups in order of effectiveness, using 1 for the group you consider most effective.

c Explain your top decision.

....
....
....
....

35 The following statements are all about the Stauffenberg bomb plot, July 1944. However, they all contain a mistake.

a Underline the mistake.
b Correct the mistake on the line below the statement.

- Claus von Stauffenberg approved of SS brutality.
  ....

- Von Stauffenberg and other army leaders created Operation Hit.
  ....

- The plan was to shoot Hitler during a meeting.
  ....

- Civilians would then take control of Berlin.
  ....

- Von Stauffenberg attended a military conference at Rastenburg. He planted the bomb under the table. During the meeting he remained in the room until the bomb exploded.
  ....

- When the bomb exploded, Hitler was killed.
  ....

- Von Stauffenberg and leading plotters were fined for their actions.
  ....

36 Complete the table to show how individuals within the church opposed the Nazi Party.

Individual	Religion	Mainly opposed to	Nazi Party reaction
Martin Niemöller			
Dietrich Bonhoeffer			

37 Define the following key terms.

Key term	Definition
Aryan	
Censorship	
Dictatorship	
Opposition	
Propaganda	
Repression	
Totalitarian	

Exam-style questions

38 Describe two problems Goebbels' propaganda and censorship policies encountered between 1933 and 1945.

5 **4 marks**

39 In what ways did opposition groups show their dissatisfaction with the Nazi regime? Explain your answer.

⏱ 10   **8 marks**

....

40 What was the more important reason for there being little opposition to the Nazi Party between 1933 and 1939? Explain your answer with reference to both factors.

⏱ 15   **12 marks**

- Nazi propaganda
- Terror and fear

Plan your answer below and write it on a separate piece of paper.

....

The experiences of Germans under the Nazis

REVISION AND PRACTICE RESOURCES
AQA GCSE (9–1) History
Workbooks

ISBN: 9781510418967   ISBN: 9781510418974   ISBN: 9781510418981   ISBN: 9781510418998   ISBN: 9781510418622

My Revision Notes

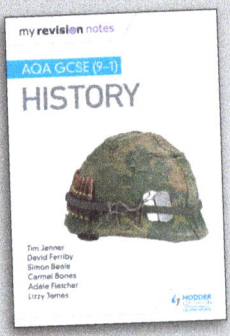

ISBN: 9781510404045

Hindsight magazine for GCSE History
Deepen knowledge • Improve skills • Achieve success

Print   eMagazine   Magazine Archive

For more information and/or to order *Hindsight* magazine, visit www.hoddereducation.co.uk/Magazines

Find out more and order online at: www.hoddereducation.co.uk/History/GCSE/AQA

Hodder Education, an Hachette UK company, Blenheim Court, George Street, Banbury, Oxfordshire OX16 5BH

Orders

Hachette UK Distribution, Hely Hutchinson Centre, Milton Road, Didcot, Oxfordshire, OX11 7HH

tel: 01235 827827

e-mail: education@hachette.co.uk

Lines are open 9.00 a.m.–5.00 p.m., Monday to Friday. You can also order through the Hodder Education website: www.hoddereducation.co.uk

© Adele Fletcher 2018

ISBN 978-1-5104-1896-7

First printed 2018

Impression number 5

Year   2023

All rights reserved; no part of this publication may be reproduced, stored in a retrieval system, or transmitted, in any form or by any means, electronic, mechanical, photocopying, recording or otherwise without either the prior written permission of Hodder Education or a licence permitting restricted copying in the United Kingdom issued by the Copyright Licensing Agency Ltd, www.cla.co.uk.

Cover photo: ullsteinbild/TopFoto

Typeset by Aptara, India

Printed in UK

Hachette UK's policy is to use papers that are natural, renewable and recyclable products and made from wood grown in well-managed forests and other controlled sources. The logging and manufacturing processes are expected to conform to the environmental regulations of the country of origin.

HODDER EDUCATION
t: 01235 827827
e: education@hachette.co.uk
w: hoddereducation.co.uk